Intricate Simplicity

Lakshmi Srikari Ravulaparthi

BookLeaf Publishing

India | USA | UK

Presentation by *BookLeaf Publishing*

Web: www.bookleafpub.com

E-mail: info@bookleafpub.com

ISBN: 9789358369311

First edition 2023

A Beautiful Blur

Dreamed reality and lived dreams the past six to twelve months,
During what now seems to be a beautiful blur.
Stranger, yet an instant connection. Although one-sided, of course.
Still vividly remember that night. Thursday, April 7, 2022, when
Amid the starlit sky, twinkling city lights, and windy night breeze,
We crossed paths.
Ever since, there was a constant battle between destiny and this- love or whatever.
Everything that reminded me of you. Signs or coincidences?
Out of the tens of thousands of people there, why did I feel such a connection with you only.
Even then, why did it only just click on that particular day?
How do I describe my exact feelings whenever I came across you since then?
Mix of ecstasy, frenzy, jitters, shyness, excitement,
But mainly magic.
My heart would start beating extremely fast in nervousness, yet

it would feel like I was flying in the clouds with
butterflies in my stomach.
Love songs started to make more sense, and
unknowingly I became the lead to a fantasy love
story created in my imagination.
Maybe in another lifetime, it did work out.

Ocean's Melody

Golden sundown,
shimmering as the ocean's music
swayed across.

Transcendence

As opaque as the moon,
Translucent as the clouds,
and
Transparent as the wind.

Love Letter to Life

To all the
early mornings, brimming with the aroma of
coffee
afternoons, radiating with the laughter of family
and friends
evenings, gleaming with the glow of sunsets
and nights, twinkling with the comfort of
moonlit sleep,
Thank you so much.

Starstruck

As I lay under the no moon sky, blanket-like and
shining with countless stars,
life suddenly seemed different.
How trivial am I, my "problems," and whatever I
go through everyday, compared to the vast
cosmos.
Here I am, an infinitesimal element of
something beyond my imagination.

Lost Puzzle

Stranded on this journey called life,
As a lone traveler,
Figuring out my way to destination.

Ink Power

Some pages
Made of paper arising from bark tree,
Would not be expected to hold the power of
sparking imagination
Which significantly impacts perspectives.
The ink from those pages
Induces visuals in the brains
To permanently stamp one's journey in life

Living in a Fairytale

Amidst this stranded place,
In this sphere of the vast universe,
Full of unknown fascinations,
A small speck of dust,
Each particle,
carries different stories and experiences.

Spooky Self

A dumbfounded girl
Walking alone in an empty, narrow hallway
While a shadow creeps up behind
Tiny, tiny footsteps,
Howling wind filling the silence
She looks behind,
Found to look at the younger reflection

Confusion of the Moment

A long device in one hand
An air pod in one ear
Clueless of the surroundings

Unforgotten Past

Horses galloping,
Soldiers marching,
Kings ruling,
Towering pyramids,
A time that can never return
Nor a time that we can travel to.

Past, Present, Future

One transportive vehicle
More than 100 individuals
Various pasts and presents
What future is in store for them?

Our Insignificance

Trillions of universes
Containing billions of galaxies
Comprising millions of stars,
Arising a new life,
Writing its small thoughts.

Inner Strength

"Hey you!"
"Loser!"
Walking through the dispiriting crowd
"Look up!" shouts a voice
From what feels distant
Yet, coming from the heart

Societal Crash

Children wailing,
While the revolting, scented dust
Infiltrated the dreary air.
October 29th, 1929,
Black Tuesday.
A date etched in history.

Into the Wild

Fresh water descending from the clouds,
Immersing through soaked pods on the river.
Birds chirping,
Snakes slithering,
Vigilant eyes watching.
Wandering the mystic rainforests of the
unknown.

Mentor

Writing on the whiteboards enthusiastically,
while traveling back in time,
seeing her younger self from twenty years ago
sitting in those same seats,
now standing in front of the classroom with
authority.
How rewarding it feels to see a classroom full of
prospective scholars.

Soulful Musings

As vivacious as a butterfly,
With a soul as intensive as the depths of the
ocean,
I am myself,
Pure, erratic, and rooted.